Hudders
FRAME by FRAME

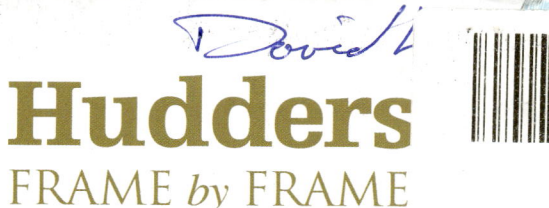

At Play	04
The Way We Worked	12
The Arts	20
Rural Life	28
Learning	34
Shopping	42
Transport	50
Sport	58
Changing Town	66
Having Fun	72

THROUGHOUT the decades Huddersfield has continually moved with the times, although not always smoothly. Despite adversity, the town has managed to retain a position as one of the most important and culturally diverse towns in the land.

Two hundred years ago Huddersfield was at the forefront of the Luddite rebellion as workers took up sledgehammers to protect their cottage woollen industry. But when the inevitable happened and mechanical looms and machines filled the newly-built factories, instead of licking their wounds and admitting defeat, they showed true Yorkshire grit by embracing the new technology to become the world's leading producers of fine quality worsted.

Today, Huddersfield has an eye to the future and a foot planted in the past. Although most of the dark satanic mills are now designer apartments and the noisy looms and mass machinery of the engineering industry have largely been silenced, entrepreneurial locals have reinvented the town as a centre of specialism, making suits for royalty, machines which can measure a speck of dust and 21st century hip joints.

The green hills which brought sheep and textiles have proved to be a jewel in Huddersfield's crown. Although the great outdoors has been abandoned by many of today's youngsters, the surrounding countryside has become a playground for a growing population and home to flourishing farm shops supplying local produce.

Through the following pages, faithfully recorded by Huddersfield Examiner photographers over the decades since the War, we take a stroll into the past together to celebrate the life and people who have helped to shape the Huddersfield of today.

Heritage Editor: Harri Aston
Written and compiled by: Linda Whitwam
Designer: Ben Renshaw

Part of the Lost Britain Collection
© 2013 Trinity Mirror. All Rights Reserved

Managing Director: Ken Rogers
Senior Editor: Steve Hanrahan
Senior Art Editor: Rick Cooke
Editor: Paul Dove
Senior Marketing Executive: Claire Brown
Photosales: 0845 300 3021
Images: Mirrorpix, PA Photos
Printed by: William Gibbons

No part of this magazine may be produced, stored in a retrieval system, or transmitted in any form, or by any means, online, electronic, mechanical, photocopying, recording or otherwise without the prior permission in writing of the copyright holders, nor be otherwise circulated in any form of binding or cover other than in which it is published and without a similar condition being imposed on a subsequent publisher.

In instances where Trinity Mirror may not own the copyright, every effort has been made to trace the original copyright holder. Any oversight will be rectified in future editions of this publication.

HUDDERSFIELD: FRAME BY FRAME

Joy of childhood Children playing in Greenhead Park, July 22, 1952

AT PLAY

The way we used to play and laugh

In the post-war period young people made up for a lack of money with imagination and enjoyed a childhood rich in memories

05

HUDDERSFIELD: FRAME BY FRAME

After the Second World War the sense of freedom was exemplified by the nation's youth. Children would count the hours to the weekend or the end of the school day when they could race outdoors to meet up with friends.

Streets, parks and playgrounds reverberated with the noisy, happy sound of them playing and running free, a time when being in a gang meant playing out with a group of pals.

Kids made up for the lack of money with a great deal of imagination and played outside for hours on end until a parent shouted from the doorstep or arrived on the scene to shepherd their youngster back home for a meal.

With little traffic, children ruled the local streets which became the venue for any game with a ball, hopscotch, Simon Says, skipping, British Bulldog, cowboys and indians, Red Rover, tag, marbles, hide and seek and a host of other popular outdoor pastimes in the 1950s and 1960s.

As well as their independent daily play, millions took part in organised activities. Many were brownies or guides, cubs or scouts. They met in church and village halls every week and went off to camp in the summer.

There were other events, such as the eagerly-anticipated village fair which gave them a chance to dress up, be part of a parade, become a carnival queen, show off their skills, win a goldfish or – even more exotic – a coconut.

Highlights of the year included Guy Fawkes Night which provided a rare money-making opportunity by dressing up a guy and asking for pennies on the pavement – a reward for all the time spent 'chumping' for bonfire wood.

At Christmas, woolly socks were hung next to the fireplace and in the morning there would be a shiny penny and an orange inside and, if the child was fortunate, a small present or two. The post-war children may not have had many material possessions but their generation enjoyed a childhood rich in memories.

▲ **Camp scene**
Scouts in Bradley Wood on May 29, 1950. The wood is now dissected by the M62 motorway

▶ **Style icons**
Children in fancy dress at Greenhead Park on July 24, 1948

AT PLAY

May Queen Mayday at Crosland Moor Infants School, May 1, 1961

Flaming success Bonfire Night, 1960

07

HUDDERSFIELD: FRAME BY FRAME

▶ **Young mechanics** Crosland Moor Boy Scouts proudly display their self-made go-kart on May 17, 1952

AT PLAY

▼ **Parade pride** Big crowds turned out at Market Place for the Scouts' parade on May 17, 1951

◀ **Learning to fly** Two boys play with a model aeroplane on Lindley Moor, August 20, 1948

▲ **Happy faces** A children's Christmas Party at Crow Edge on December 20, 1948

◀ **Help at hand** Scouts' winter competition – the first aid test, December 9, 1950

09

HUDDERSFIELD: FRAME BY FRAME

Ready for Santa Children with Christmas stockings at the fireplace, pictured on December 22, 1949

▶ **Plain sailing** Children paddling and testing out their model yachts at Ravensknowle Park on May 31 1950

AT PLAY

▶ **Remember, remember** Children having fun on Bonfire Night, 1960

▲ **Cold spring** Children with their dog, playing in the snow at Brighouse on March 7, 1949

◀ **Splashing fun** Children playing in the paddling pool in Greenhead Park on a warm and sunny July day in 1952

HUDDERSFIELD: FRAME BY FRAME

▶ *Traditional work* A woman at work in a textile mill, pictured on June 15, 1949

THE WAY WE WORKED

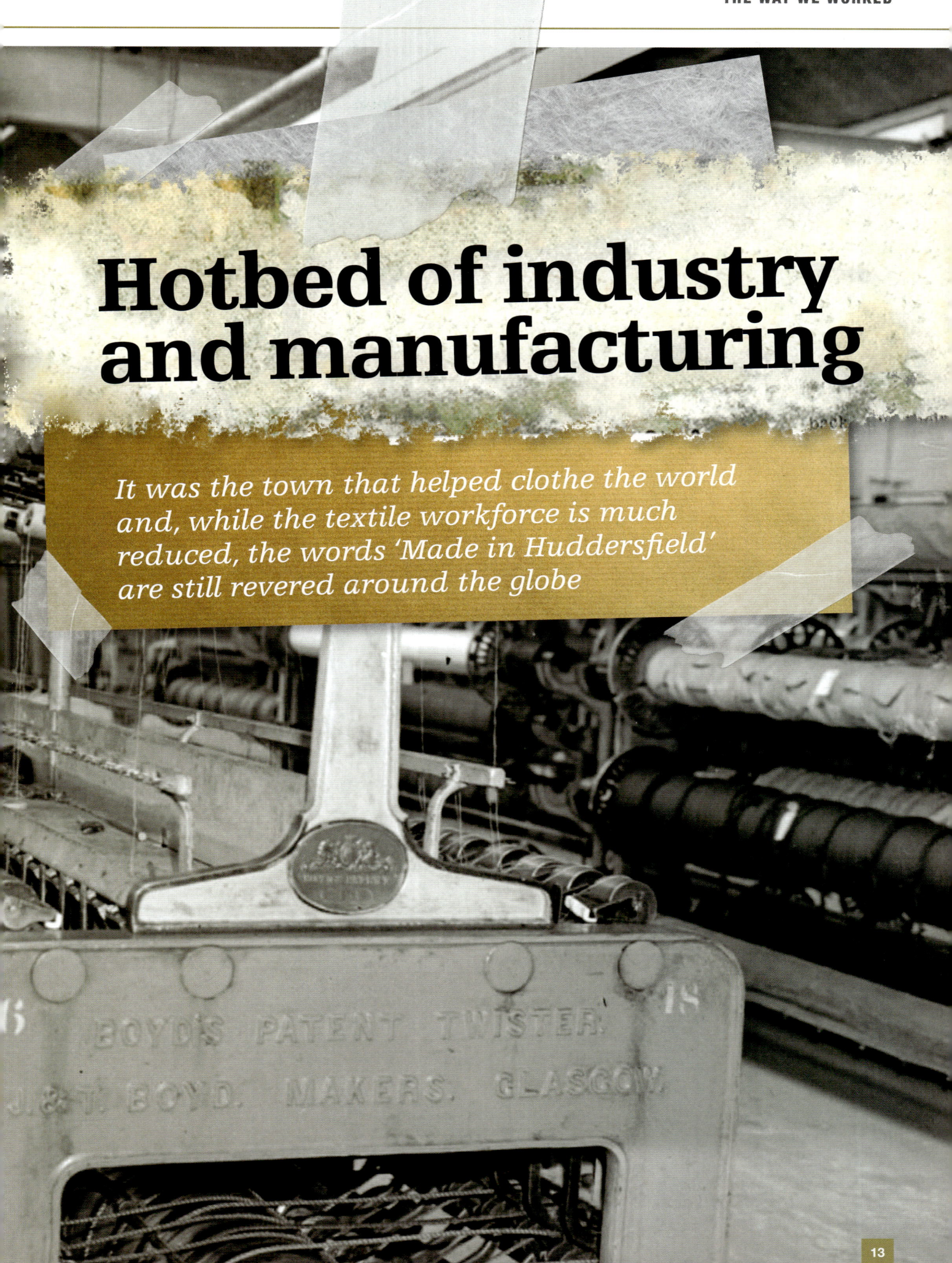

Hotbed of industry and manufacturing

It was the town that helped clothe the world and, while the textile workforce is much reduced, the words 'Made in Huddersfield' are still revered around the globe

HUDDERSFIELD: FRAME BY FRAME

▲ Good times
A mill party at James Sykes, Milnsbridge, June 1, 1953

THERE was a time when every family in Huddersfield could claim to have a relative working in the woollen mills.

The town's wealth was born out of textiles, especially high-quality worsteds, and left a legacy of fine mansions and commercial buildings, most of which still stand today.

However, the transition from weavers' cottages to dark satanic mills was not a smooth one. Huddersfield was a hotbed of Luddite rebellion, and vivid tales of murder, arson, ambushes and resistance have been handed down from generation to generation.

After the Industrial Revolution a forest of mill chimneys mushroomed in the town and valleys, belching out their thick black smoke. The post-war smogs are legendary. On bad days pedestrians struggled to see more than a few feet ahead and the polluting black mist left its sooty scar on the Millstone Grit of houses and factories.

By the 1950s textiles employed tens of thousands of people, most of whom had started work at 14. Huddersfield, along with its West Yorkshire neighbours of Bradford and Halifax, was the textile powerhouse which clothed the world. Thousands more workers were employed in Huddersfield's other two main industries of engineering and pharmaceuticals. ICI was one of the town's biggest employers and one of the 1984 original FTSE 100 Index members.

David Brown has been at the forefront of engineering for a century and a half, producing gears and, until 1988, tractors.

At its height there were more than 2,500 agents in 100 countries selling tractors made at the Meltham factory.

In those days directors had separate canteens from shopfloor workers who had to clock on and off.

The stampede through the factory gates when the end-of-shift hooter sounded was a sight to behold and a sign of the times.

Nowadays, textiles have shrunk into a highly specialised industry with a small workforce but the town continues to make cloth for royalty.

And the words 'Made in Huddersfield' woven into the selvedge of a bolt of cloth are still revered from Shrewsbury to Shanghai.

THE WAY WE WORKED

Food for thought David Brown executives head for lunch in the canteen on November 20, 1950

Outdoor worker Farmer J A Haigh feeding sheep on the moors on February 3, 1954

Youthful exuberance A young worker at David Brown's, March 6, 1950

Crystals to dye Mrs D Couchman packing dyestuff crystals at ICI Dalton Works, September 14, 1949

15

HUDDERSFIELD: FRAME BY FRAME

▶ **Well alight** A fire at a mill in Aspley on June 1, 1954

▶ **Worker's reward** A presentation at Brierleys Mill, April 24, 1952

THE WAY WE WORKED

▲ **Skilled** A textile worker at Skelmanthorpe, July 17, 1953

▲ **Looking good** Fashion designer and royal dressmaker Norman Hartnell at Kagan Textiles in May 1962

◀ **Aiming high** Preparing the rockets for Bonfire Night in 1950 at Standard Fireworks

HUDDERSFIELD: FRAME BY FRAME

▶ **Industrial stalwart** William Whiteley's engineers of textile and machine tools were employing 500 people at this time in Lockwood, July 15, 1954

▲ **No day off** Office workers, pictured on New Year's Day in 1951 – it was not designated a bank holiday until 1974

◀ **Place of work** The Imperial Chemical Industries yard, December 11, 1948

THE WAY WE WORKED

Don't lose the thread A textiles mill worker pictured on June 15, 1949

Warping skills Future Colne Valley MP Richard Wainwright, centre, at the mill of C and J Hirst on June 6, 1960

Back-breaking work Workers at a paper mill in Outlane, December 1, 1953

HUDDERSFIELD: FRAME BY FRAME

▸ **Top hat** Waring Green Players' performance of Wanted As One Body in Brighouse on April 29, 1962

THE ARTS

Turning spotlight on talented performers

The Huddersfield calendar is peppered with artistic events throughout the year, giving local people a chance to show their talents

Huddersfield has a vibrant and eclectic arts scene. It takes in the whole spectrum of the arts and operates at every level, from the internationally famous Huddersfield Choral Society to community choirs with age ranges from six to 86, from amateur dramatic and operatic groups to famous actors, hobby creative writers to best-selling authors, scribblers of limericks to leading poets and from local dance troupes to Royal Ballet stars.

The town's calendar is peppered with annual events such as the Holmfirth Arts Festival, the Mrs Sunderland Music Festival, Huddersfield Literary Festival and Marsden Jazz Festival, to name but a few, which give local residents and those from further afield the chance to showcase their talents.

While the arts continue to be an important means of self expression, in the days before ubiquitous television sets and internet access they also provided the main form of community entertainment.

Church and village halls across the borough were bursting to the seams with audiences eager to see Brighouse's Waring Green Players or Longwood Chapel Society perform their latest play, and parks and streets were packed with families straining to catch a better glimpse of the marching brass bands.

Hundreds would attend the annual Longwood Sing, a 140-year-old communal singing event which survives to this day.

The town and its villages have always had a strong tradition of music in schools and over the decades they have produced fine musicians whose reputations have spread far beyond Britain's shores.

The Huddersfield Choral Society, dating back to 1836, is synonymous with the town. The 200 members' unique full-bodied 'Huddersfield Sound' is renowned across the world. They have made numerous recordings and their Hymns Album reached number eight in the UK Album Chart in 1986. On December 16, 1953, they made history by starring in the first TV broadcast of their signature Handel's Messiah, transmitted from Huddersfield Town Hall with conductor Sir Malcolm Sargent.

▲ **Street parade**
A brass military band parading through Ramsden Street, Huddersfield, on September 26, 1961

THE ARTS

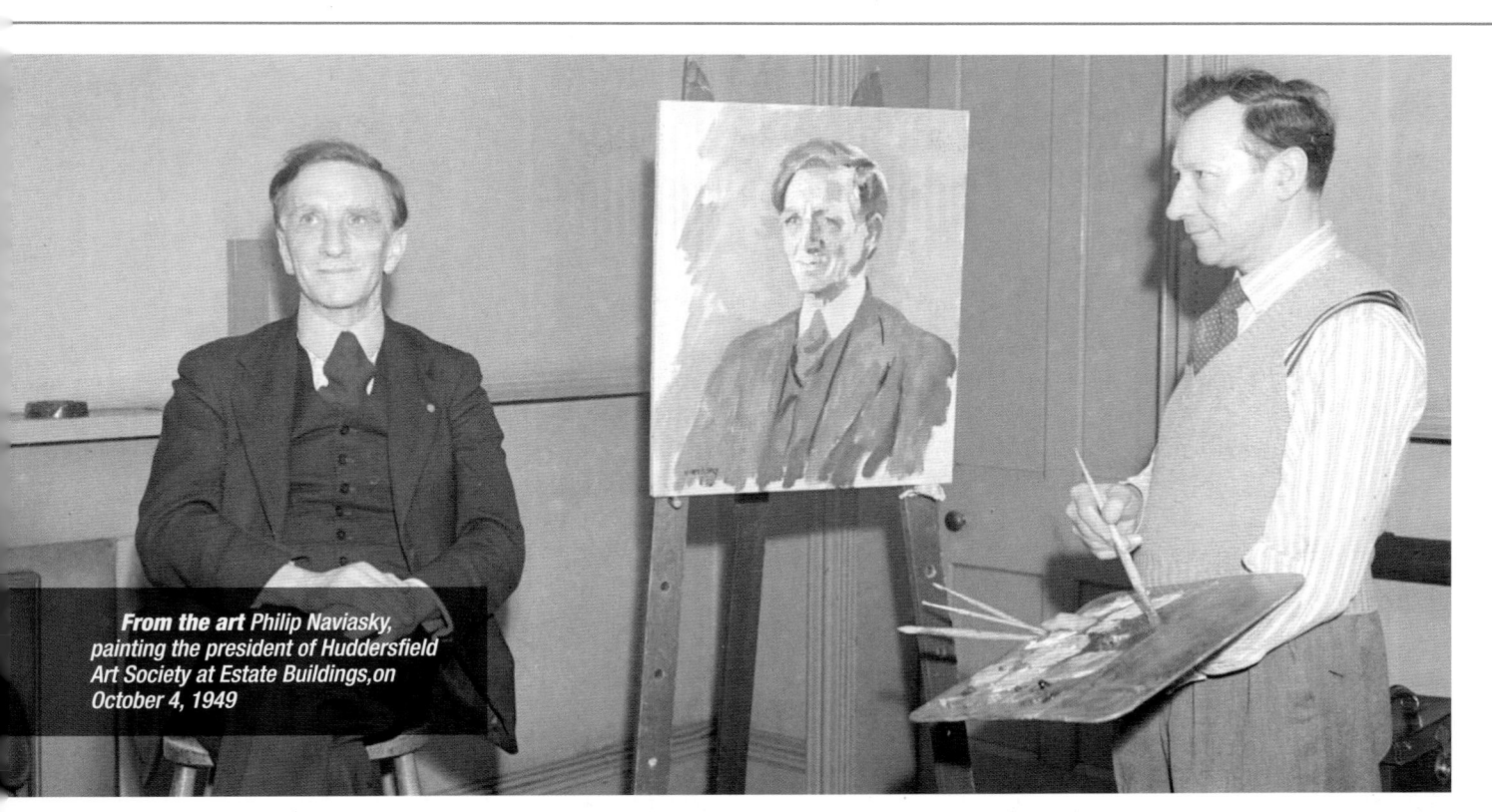

From the art Philip Naviasky, painting the president of Huddersfield Art Society at Estate Buildings, on October 4, 1949

Costume drama Pink Champagne by Longwood Society, October 7, 1950

HUDDERSFIELD: FRAME BY FRAME

▲ **Take note**
Choral Society members get ready to perform Handel's Messiah, December 8, 1962

▶ **Stage show**
Longwood Chapel Society's Wild Violets, pictured on September 30, 1953

THE ARTS

Showtime Here We Come Gathering, a play by Philip King and Anthony Armstrong, staged by Waring Green Players on February 20, 1962

Competitive music Musicians competing in a brass band contest on May 15, 1960

Take a bow Violinists at the Mrs Sunderland Music Festival on February 12, 1949

HUDDERSFIELD: FRAME BY FRAME

▲ **Keyboard man** Richard Wood at Woods Music Shop on October 1, 1962

▶ **Taking a break** Brass band contest at Greenhead Park, July 29, 1961

◀ **Fine dress** A scene from a pantomime in Mirfield on January 5, 1951

THE ARTS

Hands up Pigeon Pie by Waring Green Players, Brighouse, in February 1960

Make-up magic Longwood Chapel Society members prepare for a performance of Wild Voilets in 1953

HUDDERSFIELD: FRAME BY FRAME

Family affair
Haymaking at Lower Hey Farm, July 26, 1951

RURAL LIFE

A taste of rural life is on our doorstep

The countryside and the number of viable farms may have shrunk but the link between town and country remains strong, with our agricultural shows as popular as ever

HUDDERSFIELD: FRAME BY FRAME

▲ **Unusual pet** Elaine Smith with pet pigs at Fern Grove Farm, Brackenhall, on August 16, 1954

People who don't know Huddersfield think of it as an industrial town. But that's only half the story.

Textiles and engineering flourished in the Colne and Holme Valleys and around the town centre but inbetween the factories and houses were, and still are, mile after mile of greenery – home to dozens of traditional livestock farms – which rise up to the bleak Pennine moorland peppered with sheep.

The countryside and the number of viable farms may have shrunk but the link between town and country is as strong as ever. Although we no longer see men wheeling milk churns along dusty village roads, Huddersfield is one of the last places in the country where you can still have green top (unpasteurised) milk delivered, supplied by farms not a stone's throw away from your front doorstep.

And today the town and surrounding villages are blessed with an unrivalled range of first-class farm shops providing wonderfully fresh produce where the food miles travelled from pasture to plate can be measured in single figures.

The days when horses pulled ploughs are long gone but there are more horses and ponies than ever in Huddersfield. Our equine friends have firmly established themselves as a popular pastime and an integral part of semi-rural life here.

In the fields, hay is gathered with tractors and balers instead of pitchforks these days but, if you travel along a country road on a fine summer's night there is a good chance you'll still see local lads – and lasses – helping to gather in the hay and silage.

Honley, Emley and Penistone Agricultural Shows are thriving and competition for Best in Show is still as fierce as ever among local farmers, just as it was between their ancestors. Penistone Show is more than 140 years old and, if today's popularity is anything to go by, it will still be here long after we are gone.

RURAL LIFE

◀ **Feeding time** A farmer with a young pig on November 10, 1953

◀ **Traditional travel** Horse and carriage at Lowerhouses in April 1953

HUDDERSFIELD: FRAME BY FRAME

▶ **Hold on tight** Children on a horse at Nor Brook Farm, January 16, 1953

▶ **Harvest work** Loading corn at Bracken Hall Farm, Mirfield, August 14, 1952

RURAL LIFE

▶ **Farm pest** Jean Mate with a fox at Windsor Farm, Blackmoorfoot, on November 16, 1948

▲ **All ready** A scene from Honley Show on June 13, 1949

▶ **Pat on the back** Pig-keeping at Martins Mill, Lindley, August 25, 1953

▲ **Young lambs** A boy with lambs at a Hove Edge farm on March 16, 1962

HUDDERSFIELD: FRAME BY FRAME

Leaving a lasting mark on our lives

Schools have changed a great deal over the decades but, for many of us, they remain the places where we spent some of the best days of our lives

LEARNING

at school.
to come to school.

Early learning Dalton County Primary School, January 17, 1949. The stove heater is encased in a chicken wire cage for safety

HUDDERSFIELD: FRAME BY FRAME

Many of us remember our schooldays as some of the happiest times of our life.

Cold, draughty classrooms with hard, wooden chairs at ancient desks with countless initials carved into them, itchy school uniforms three sizes too big because "you'll grow into them," the stern expressions of some teachers, lukewarm free school milk and the unappetising aroma of school dinners all disappear into the mists of time as we recall those simple, carefree days of our youth with a smile.

Some things we learned as children are still carried with us today and some of the friendships we made in class have lasted a lifetime.

Other classmates are no longer with us but their memory still burns brightly as we remember those black and white days in vivid Technicolor.

Huddersfield has a long-standing reputation for fine schools and innovation in education. In the 1950s and 1960s the grammar schools led the academic way. Two of them were King James', founded in 1547 and today one of the country's top comprehensive schools, and Greenhead High School for Girls which became the prestigious Greenhead College, a national leader in sixth form education.

In 1965 the town was one of the first places in the country to embrace the comprehensive education system, opening purpose-built schools like Colne Valley to provide new opportunities for thousands of local youngsters.

Between them Huddersfield's schools have produced men and women who have gone on to make their mark in science, the arts, sport and politics throughout the world. One such man was former Royds Hall Grammar School pupil Harold Wilson, British prime minister from 1964 to 1970 and again from 1974 to 1976.

His schoolmates remember him as a confident young man who blithely told them he was going to become prime minister one day. Sometimes school day dreams really do come true.

▲ **Learning environment** *A classroom scene from Holme Valley Grammar School, April 7, 1954*

▶ **Choir practice** *Royds Hall Grammar School, March 2, 1954*

LEARNING

Royal visit With Princess Elizabeth and the Duke of Edinburgh on their way, children at Waverley School are ready for the visitors on July 26, 1949

Note perfect A Holme Valley Grammar School music lesson in April, 1954

37

HUDDERSFIELD: FRAME BY FRAME

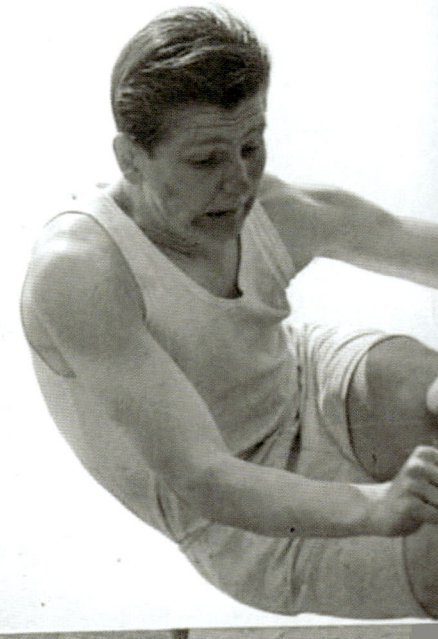

▶ **Learning new skills** Enrolling for a new term at Huddersfield Technical College on September 15, 1954

▼ **Ready for industry** Pupils put their technical skills into practice at Royds Hall on March 2, 1954

LEARNING

High achiever A scene from Royds Hall's sports day, June 1, 1960

On track A hurdler competing at Huddersfield New College's sports day on July 11, 1961

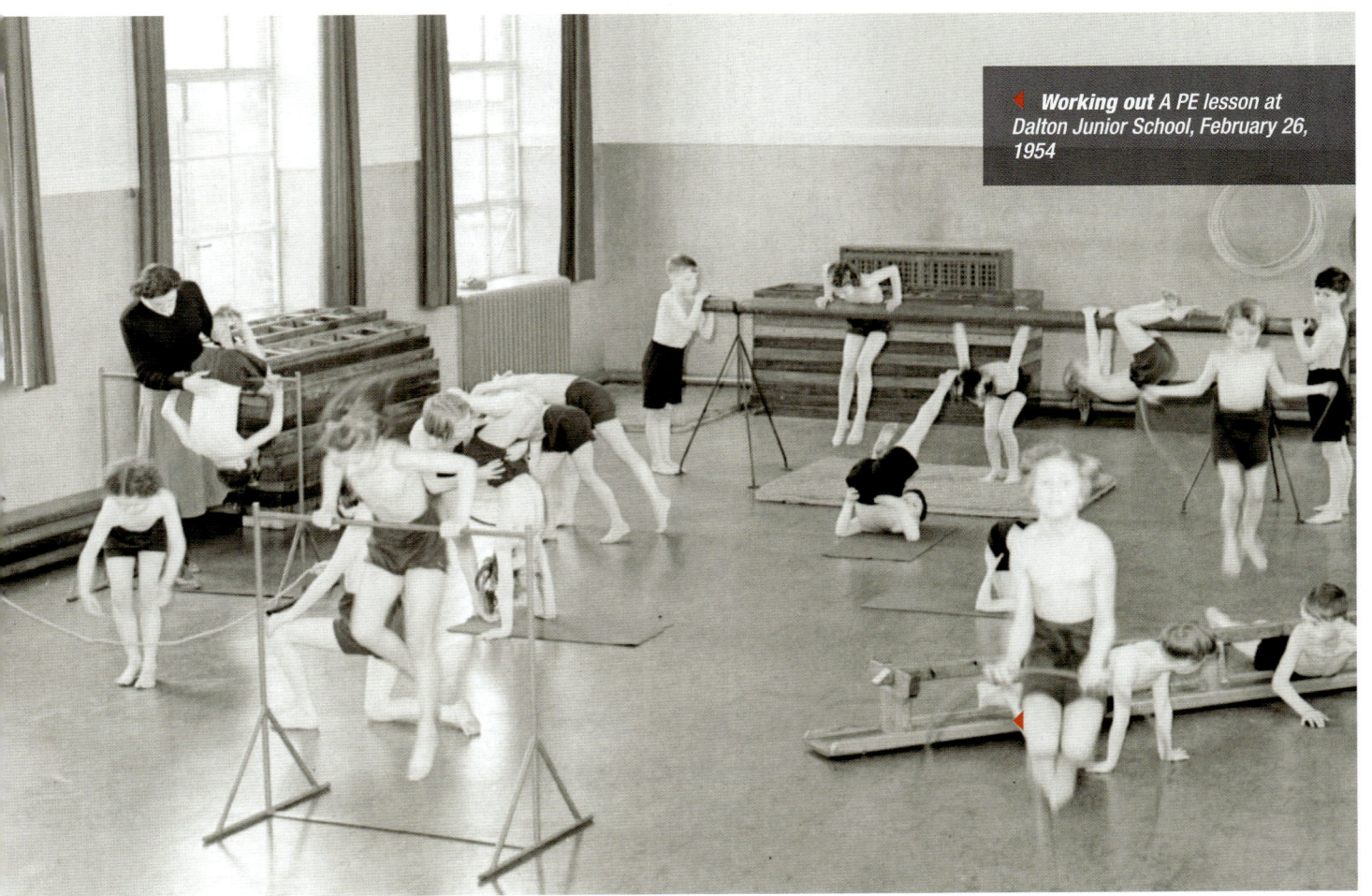

Working out A PE lesson at Dalton Junior School, February 26, 1954

HUDDERSFIELD: FRAME BY FRAME

LEARNING

▲ **Science students**
Chemistry lessons at Royds Hall School, March 2, 1954

▶ **Merry men**
Almondbury Grammar School children and their Robin Hood show, July 4, 1952

The Huddersfield Daily Examiner

All Our Yesterdays

Our readers love nostalgia which is why we have some in every edition of the Examiner with our Memory Lane photographs on the letters page. We also publish our ever-popular eight-page nostalgia supplement All Our Yesterdays every Wednesday which also includes a special local history feature on its back page every week.

EVERY WEDNESDAY

LOVE YOUR HISTORY?
LOVE HUDDERSFIELD

Are you an expert on local history? Can you give the lowdown on things like Huddersfield's historic buildings or how the textiles industry helped shape the town? If you have knowledge of any specific heritage subject, please get in touch and play a part in Britain's biggest-ever media heritage project. With your support, we will be bringing history back to life...

E-mail the Heritage Editor:
harri.aston@trinitymirror.com

LOST HUDDERSFIELD

HUDDERSFIELD: FRAME BY FRAME

Look back on the way we shopped

It may once have been an almost daily chore but many still remember with fondness the days before supermarkets and online shopping

▶ **Last-minute bargains** Shoppers in the Shambles, on Christmas Eve, 1952

SHOPPING

HUDDERSFIELD: FRAME BY FRAME

Local shops
A view of Market Hall, Shambles and the Unicorn Pub from the top of Huddersfield Library, captured on October 31, 1953

Before the days of refrigerators, freezers and microwaves, shopping was an almost daily chore.

The streets in the centre of Huddersfield were throng with housewives buying groceries and pausing to gaze in wonder at the new-fangled televisions and wirelesses in the town's showrooms. In October 1952 the first zebra crossing was introduced and on Saturdays it was so busy that it had to be manned full-time by a rota of police officers.

One of the most popular shopping areas was the Shambles, near the current pedestrianised walkway leading from WH Smith to the Piazza. Little is known of its origins but we do know it dates back to the 1770s.

It is thought that the original tradesmen were butchers but older residents will remember the Shambles as a pre-supermarket one-stop shop where they could buy everything from flowers to flour and fruit and veg, meat, fish and a host of other goods.

For those who didn't want to make the time-consuming trolleybus ride into the centre, there were always a good range of well-stocked local shops. Every village and district had its own butcher, grocer, greengrocer and general store at the very least.

Then there were the men who travelled around in vans catering for working women, stopping outside their factories and homes with bread, groceries, meat, fish and chips and other essentials.

There was great excitement when the Lodges family opened Huddersfield's first 'hypermarket' in the 1960s and shoppers flocked to fill their (by today's standards) tiny trolleys with tinned peaches and other exotic foodstuffs.

During the same decade cars began to become more common and, in July 1966, the first eight traffic wardens went on duty in Huddersfield town centre.

Two months later shopkeepers were already describing them as 'over zealous' – a theme which still resonates today with town centre traders.

SHOPPING

▲ **Customer service** Plenty of shop assistants were on hand when this picture was snapped on December 13, 1960

◀ **Street scene** Buxton Road (now High Street), Huddersfield, March 3, 1947

▶ **Bread delivery** Finding the time to get to the shops was a difficulty experienced by many married women working in the mills and factories. The Huddersfield Co-op organised a bread delivery van to visit Blamires and other mills at lunchtime. It is pictured here at Blamires on November 4, 1948

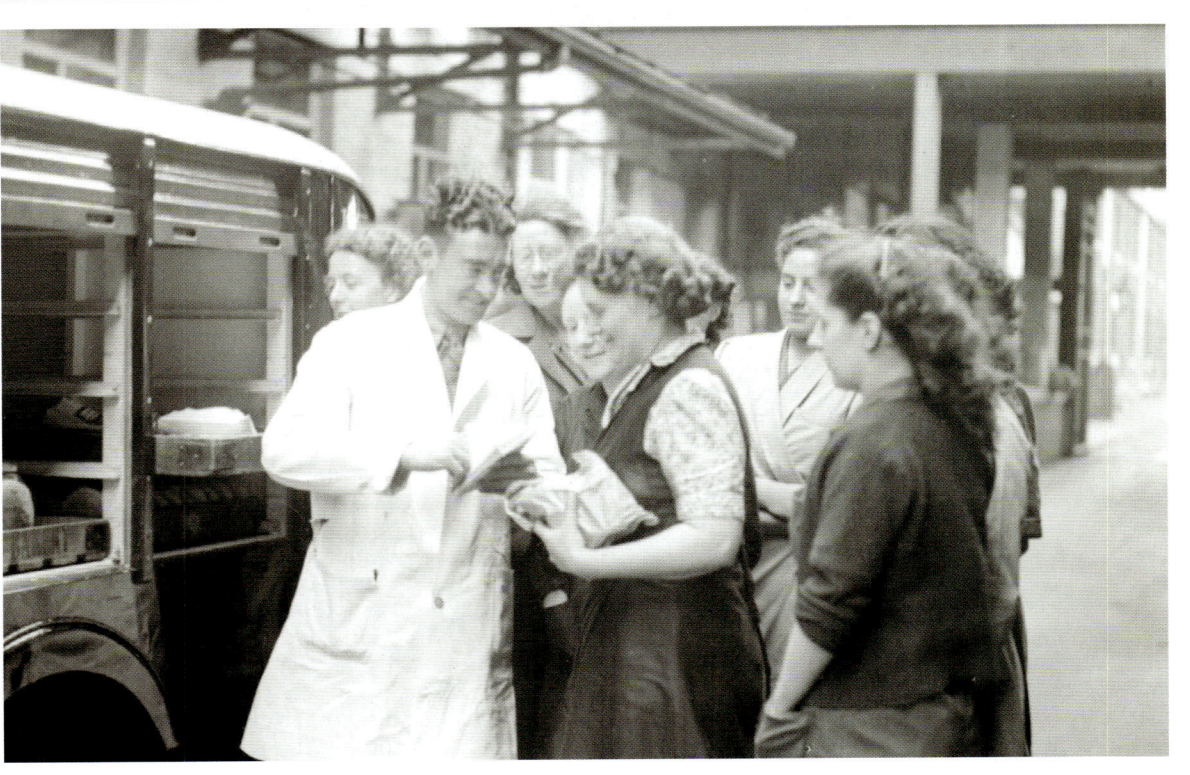

HUDDERSFIELD: FRAME BY FRAME

▲ **Latest technology**
Television sales were on the increase in the mid-1950s. This photo was taken at Clydesdale Radio and Television shop, Queen Street, November 15, 1954

▶ **Right at home**
The opening of NCB Showroom on October 25, 1961

SHOPPING

◀ **Independent style**
An Elland shopkeeper on July 2, 1953

▲ **Fancy some sweets?**
A shop at Outlane, Emley, on November 5, 1963

▼ **Showbiz glamour** Pat Phoenix, star of TV show Coronation Street, cut the opening ribbon of this new shop on Queen Street on March 3, 1962

47

HUDDERSFIELD: FRAME BY FRAME

▶ **Cut above**
A butchers' shop in Huddersfield, July 9, 1954

▶ **Retail revolution**
Patricia Ball at a Honley shop on September 11, 1962

SHOPPING

◀ **Building bigger** New, larger buildings taking shape behind shops at Milnsbridge on May 20, 1954, revealing the state of things to come

▶ **So much choice** Market shoppers at Shambles Lane, Huddersfield, on September 27, 1946

▶ **Children's delight** Toy stall in Market Hall, December 19, 1952

◀ **Taking shape** Huddersfield's New Market Hall under construction in 1968

49

HUDDERSFIELD: FRAME BY FRAME

▶ **Up to speed**
Anne Hall and Mary Newton, the famous sisters who raced in the 1950s, are pictured here on June 12, 1951

TRANSPORT

Hop on board for journey into past

Today, cars rule the roads but many people still long for the return of Huddersfield's much-missed trolleybuses

51

HUDDERSFIELD: FRAME BY FRAME

▲ **Dignitaries line up** *The last trolleybus is given a grand send-off in 1968*

JULY 13, 1968, marked the end of an era for Huddersfield. The journey from Waterloo to Outlane on that day was the very last that a trolleybus would make in the town.

This popular mode of transport was phased out in favour of the diesel engine after just 35 years and enthusiasts came from all over England to mark the occasion.

Public transport was already beginning to wane as the public began its love affair with the motor car. Town centre car showrooms like Volvo dealer Olaf Olsen proudly displayed their latest luxury offerings which at around £1,500 in the mid-1960s were way beyond most working people's pocket.

A few managed to scrape together the £550 or so for an economical new Morris Minor but mostly the new generation of motorists patched together old vehicles and rode round in what would today be classed as old bangers.

Oil leaks were normal, steering problems were common, mechanical failures were part and parcel of car ownership and even wheels falling off en route were not unknown. It was all part of the thrilling new experience known as motoring, and two Huddersfield women, Anne and Mary – the "mad Newton sisters" – of Newton's Motor Engineers, Viaduct Street, took the rally scene by storm.

Ex-Greenhead High School girl Anne (Hall after marriage) was a highly skilled and extremely fast driver who won several major trophies, including the Ladies' Cup at the 1953 London Motor Rally and the coveted Coupe des Dames at Monte Carlo in 1961.

Travelling by train was a more sedate affair and many travellers will remember with fondness the wonderful steam locomotives which used to fill the valleys with their huge clouds of grey vapour as they majestically made their way from village to village, stopping at stations now long gone.

With today's soaring fuel prices and talk of carbon footprints, many local transport enthusiasts are hoping that Huddersfield will some day reintroduce the much-missed trolleybus.

TRANSPORT

Last trip The trolleybus' final journey from Marsden in 1963

▼ **Great service** Mona Lockwood, conductress on the last Huddersfield trolleybus. She had worked on the trolley busses since the Second World War and retired in 1982

▶ **Road drama** A car accident at Fartown on December 31, 1948

▶ **Coach trip** People queuing for the coach to London on Venn Street, August 6, 1948

HUDDERSFIELD: FRAME BY FRAME

▲ **End of the line** The last regular passenger train at Meltham station. Mr S Trowman, the former stationmaster, shakes hands with the driver, April 25, 1949

▶ **Free lunch** A dog receives a bone from a member of the kitchen staff on board a train at Huddersfield station on April 8, 1954

TRANSPORT

▲ **Holiday hopes** Family waiting for a train at Longwood station, October 10, 1960. British Rail posters advertise trips to holiday destinations on the notice board behind

▼ **Day trippers** Queue for Scarborough train and a day out, May 23, 1961

◀ **Traditional scene** A steam train passes through Bradley on June 18, 1953

HUDDERSFIELD: FRAME BY FRAME

Showpiece
A new Volvo sports car outside the Olaf Olsen showroom on March 9, 1962

Speedy travel
Bus to Berry Brow overtaking a sports car, on August 8, 1949

Vintage cars
Jaguar XK120 vehicles pictured outside Newton's on November 6, 1951

TRANSPORT

Recovery operation The aftermath of a car crashing into a ravine on Buckstones Moss, January 31, 1949

Fare ride During a transport strike in October 1949, people managed to pick up lifts from private motorists, as seen here in New Street

HUDDERSFIELD: FRAME BY FRAME

Good catch
A football match at Leeds Road Playing Fields on January 16, 1960

SPORT

Sport's place at heart of our lives

The birthplace of rugby league, Huddersfield has a long and proud sporting tradition dating back to the turn of the last century

HUDDERSFIELD: FRAME BY FRAME

▲ **All smiles**
Huddersfield Town coach A Young gives advice to footballers on Leeds Road, Huddersfield, August 3, 1948

SPORT has woven its way into the fabric of Huddersfield, becoming an integral part of life in the town.

Walk through any of the picturesque villages and districts on a weekend and you'll witness cricketers, bowlers, golfers, tennis players, runners, footballers and rugby players plying their trade, as their ancestors did before them.

The town has a long and proud sporting tradition dating back to the turn of the last century.

Huddersfield is the birthplace of rugby league and its memorable Team Of All Talents was unbeatable during the years before and after the First World War, resurging in 1953 to claim the Challenge Cup.

Huddersfield Town AFC's glory days were the mid-1920s, lifting the FA Cup in 1922 and becoming the first club to claim the Football League title three years running.

Two of the town's most famous sons and daughters were Derek Ibbotson and Anita Lonsbrough. Derek, the product of a fine tradition of local harriers, went on to achieve international fame by setting a new world record for the mile in 1957.

Anita, a treasurer's clerk at Huddersfield Town Hall, set five world records and won seven gold medals, including Gold in the 200m Breaststroke at the 1960 Rome Olympics. Four years later she had the honour of being Britain's first woman flag bearer at the Olympics.

Huddersfield's local sportsmen and women will never reach these dizzy heights but not even the harsh Pennine weather can dampen their love of sport.

With true Yorkshire grit, they will continue to give their all to claim their place in Huddersfield's sporting history.

SPORT

▶ **Silver lining** Bradley United Football Club with a shield and cup after a successful season, pictured on May 13, 1948

▲ **Local rivals** Runners involved in a Huddersfield College v Almondbury sporting event July 13, 1953

▲ **Strike partnership** The opening batsmen come out for the Lumb Cup Final on July 8, 1961

▶ **Impressive backdrop** The matches at Leeds Road Playing Fields with the hills rising in the background, January 16, 1960

HUDDERSFIELD: FRAME BY FRAME

▲ **Star runner**
Derek Ibbotson, a bronze medal winner in the 5,000m at the Melbourne Olympics in 1956, is pictured here with the police team at the Borough Police Gala on July 25, 1962

▶ **Prize-giving**
Athletes at Greenhead Park on July 22, 1961

SPORT

▶ **Teeing up** Bobby Locke, a four-time Open champion, and Malcolm Lee (right) at Crosland Heath Golf Club on August 26, 1951

▼ **Passing game** Rugby players pictured on March 30, 1949

◀ **Bowling competition** Bowls at the ICI works, Leeds Road, on May 26, 1953

◀ **Big draw** The Huddersfield Amateur Bowls Association Merit Final attracted a huge crowd on October 1, 1960

HUDDERSFIELD: FRAME BY FRAME

▲ **Swimming star** Huddersfield swimmer Anita Lonsbrough is pictured with her Olympic gold medal at her triumphant homecoming on September 1, 1960

▲ **High flyer** Miss B M Savage, the winner of women's high jump at the Technical College Sports Day on May 26, 1949

▶ **Punching power** Peter Smith boxing at Cambridge Road Baths, December 19, 1951

▼ **Court date** The tennis courts were busy at Greenhead Park on May 26, 1953

SPORT

▼ **Hard training** Boxers working out at Milnsbridge County Boxing Gym on New Year's Day, 1951

▲ **Hard-fought contest** Fartown v St Helens on April 6, 1953

◀ **Boxing Day hunt** Rockwood Harriers at the Junction Inn, Denby Dale, on December 26, 1961

HUDDERSFIELD: FRAME BY FRAME

Proud display
Westgate in 1951 as Royal Air Force cadets band marched past

CHANGING TOWN

Changing face of Huddersfield

The 1960s saw sweeping changes to the town's architecture, although thousands of historic buildings are still standing today

HUDDERSFIELD: FRAME BY FRAME

There was a time when it was said that Huddersfield had more Rolls-Royces per head of population than anywhere else in the world.

But the town's prosperity, built on the back of its world-renowned textile industry, turned out to be a mixed blessing for some of its finest buildings.

Unlike its less well-off neighbour Halifax, which couldn't afford to replace the 18th century Piece Hall, Huddersfield's planners were awash with schemes for brand new buildings in the 1960s – and the town had the cash to build them.

The historic 1880 Market Hall, a classic example of grandiose Victorian architecture, closed on March 31, 1970 to be replaced by the state-of-the-art concrete market hall and piazza, built between 1968 and 1970.

Architecture fans extol the virtues of its barn-like roof – the first of its kind in Europe – and curving concrete shells but these remain largely unnoticed by shoppers who have yet to forgive the council for demolishing the much-loved old Market Hall and 18th century Shambles shopping street.

The 1960s saw other sweeping changes to the town's architecture. Ramsden Street's Theatre Royal, dating back to the 1840s, staged a final production of Sailor Beware before being knocked down in February 1961. The following month the latest example of Huddersfield's civic enterprise – Huddersfield Fire Station – was opened by the mayor, Alderman Day.

Huddersfield Royal Infirmary opened its Lindley doors to the first patients in 1965, replacing the outdated infirmary on New North Road.

The town's saving grace was its sheer volume of listed buildings. With almost 3,000, Huddersfield has the third highest concentration in England. That architectural gem the Grade I neo-classical railway station, built by local firm Joseph Kaye in the mid-1800s, is one of 221 listed buildings in the town centre alone.

Nobody arriving into the town by train can fail to be impressed by the superb stone structure entered via a Corinthian portico flanked by six monumental columns and described by Sir John Betjeman as "the most splendid station facade in England."

▲ **Public service** *The seemingly chaotic scenes at the counter of the General Post Office, Northumberland Street, on December 17, 1954*

CHANGING TOWN

▸ **Towering ambition** New flats amidst old slums in Northgate on May 8, 1961

▸ **Horse power** Horse and cart outside the Huddersfield Examiner offices in Ramsden Street in 1952

▴ **Health improvements** The new hospital being built at Lindley on November 15, 1961

HUDDERSFIELD: FRAME BY FRAME

◀ **Austerity Britain**
New Street pictured in the immediate post-war period on April 25, 1948

◀ **Mail order** A mother and child using the new stamp machine on Cloth Hall Street on July 2, 1953

◀ **Garden work** The garden near St Paul's Church, Ramsden Street, January 12, 1950

CHANGING TOWN

◀ **Royal visit**
Princess Elizabeth and the Duke of Edinburgh on Ramsden Street, July 26, 1949

▼ **Boys in blue**
Police outside Ralph Cuthbert's Westgate store on August 27, 1948

▲ **Tanks again** An unfamiliar sight even during wartime, this Comet tank was on its way to the Drill Hall on Ramsden Street in October 1948

HUDDERSFIELD: FRAME BY FRAME

▶ Pedestrian priority *Zebra crossings appear in Huddersfield for the first time on New Street, pictured on January 18, 1952*

CHANGING TOWN

◀ **Cold and damp** Albert Street in 1947 with tightly-packed terraced housing

▲ **Victorian architecture** Railway Street from Market Street in April 1948

▲ **Building the future** The roundabout at the junction of Northumberland Street and Northgate, captured on April 1, 1961

▶ **Shock of the new** A view of the roundabout from Richmond Flats on July 18, 1963

73

HUDDERSFIELD: FRAME BY FRAME

▶ **Smiles of fun** Two youngsters enjoy a fun fair game at Honley on September 24, 1962

HAVING FUN

Funfairs, galas and agricultural shows

Huddersfield has a rich tradition of events for the entire community to enjoy, not only in the town itself but in the surrounding villages and countryside

HUDDERSFIELD: FRAME BY FRAME

▲ Momentous day *People awaiting a Royal visit, Ramsden Street, on July 26, 1949*

EVERYBODY loves a celebration. The town gala, village fair, local agricultural show, carnival, annual works do and the funfair – which has been coming to Leeds Road for as long as anyone can remember – all help to bind us together as a community. They give us a common cause to enjoy ourselves.

Both before and after the Second World War these rituals were an important part of the local annual calendar. Families looked forward for weeks to the annual gala, a time for old and young alike to forget about the daily grind and let their hair down.

Huddersfield has a rich tradition of these events, not only in the town itself but in the surrounding villages and countryside.

Golcar, Brighouse, Deighton, Lindley, Upperthong, Emley, Honley and Mirfield are just a few of the places where residents work for months to organise their annual community celebration.

One of the oldest is Ravensknowle Gala which celebrated its Diamond Jubilee in 1987 and is still going strong today. It originated in 1927 to provide free teas for the less well-off in the neighbourhood.

After a period in the mid-1980s when it nearly didn't take place due to lack of support, like many similar galas around Huddersfield, Ravensknowle Gala has been rejuvenated and continues to go from strength to strength as people's pride in their neighbourhood is rekindled.

The highlight of many carnivals was the procession around the streets, often on the back of a bumpy trailer, with the festival queen and her entourage taking pride of place.

Whatever the weather, people turned out in their hundreds.

Children and animals were washed and scrubbed, and mothers spent countless nights painstakingly sewing carnival queen and fancy dress costumes to make sure their youngsters looked their best.

As the multicultural Deighton Carnival of today shows, some things never change.

HAVING FUN

Naked ambition 'Lady Godiva' leads the Outlane Carnival parade on a horse, July 5, 1952

Puppy power Summer entertainment at Greenhead Park on July 19, 1952

Dog's life Mirfield Show on July 11, 1953, and a boy makes a new friend

Blooming display Rastrick Gala, July 26, 1952

77

HUDDERSFIELD: FRAME BY FRAME

▲ **Horsing around** Canker Lane Gala, Leeds Road, July 11, 1953

▲ **Centre of attention** Dalton's gala queen on July 7, 1953

◀ **Sail on** A boat on display at the David Brown Gala Day on June 13, 1952

HAVING FUN

Royal display The retiring queen and her attendants at Hade Edge Gala on July 17, 1954

Queen for the day Dalton Gala Crowning of the queen at Ravensknowle Children's Gala July 14, 1951

Dancing shoes These young children strut their stuff at the Ravensknowle Children's Gala on July 14, 1951

79

HUDDERSFIELD: FRAME BY FRAME

▶ **Boys' toys** These boys admire a weapon on display at Mirfield Show on July 9, 1960

▶ **Motor power** Children enjoy a tractor ride at the David Brown Gala Day on June 14, 1952

HAVING FUN

Swinging time ICI Gala Day, Leeds Road, June 26, 1954

Howdy, partner Children dressed up as cowboys at Linthwaite Carnival on June 14, 1952

For the kids Ravensknowle Children's Gala, July 8, 1961

Taken for a ride ICI Children's Gala, July 8, 1949

81

PURCHASE ANY PHOTO FROM THIS MAGAZINE

PHOTOGRAPHS

7x5
9x6
10x8
10x12

AVAILABLE FROM
£9.50 EACH
+£1.95 P&P

PERFECT GIFT FOR YOUR LOVED ONE

PHOTO SALES

If you would like to purchase a print featured within this publication contact our photosales team on

0845 300 3021